SUPER STRUCTURES

By Paula Goepfert

CONTENTS

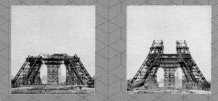

SUPER STRUCTURES

PREDICT

What information do you think you might find out about super structures?

For centuries, people have been building roads, bridges and tunnels. In that time, they have met many challenges. They have built high in the air and deep beneath the earth and water. They have built across, around, underneath and above immovable, impassable obstacles. They have faced high winds, rushing water and extremes of heat and cold as they built. And, time and again, they have found a way.

Super structures are designed and built by engineers to solve super problems. The first thing engineers think about when planning a structure is choosing the best possible location. They ask questions about the ground on which they are building. Is it rocky or swampy or sandy? They ask questions about the weather and any possible natural disasters. Will the structure have to stand up to severe storms or earthquakes or extreme temperatures?

Engineers often discover problems while studying a location. The location may not be ideal, but the structure must be built where it is needed, so the engineers have to come up with innovative solutions.

The Sydney Harbour Bridge in Australia is the widest bridge in the world. It was designed and built to link the north and south shores of the city of Sydney. It was completed in 1932 and is approximately 503 m long and 48.8 m wide.

CLARIFY

innovative

INFERENCE

What can you infer about the type of skills an engineer might need to do their job?

. . . designed and built by engineers to
solve super problems

The Eiffel Tower in France was designed and built to mark the centennial celebrations of the French Revolution. It was completed in 1889 and is 322 m high. It was the tallest structure in the world until 1930.

The Great Wall of China is the longest structure in the world. It was designed and built to protect the people of northern China from invading nomadic tribes. It was completed in the 17th century and is approximately 7240 km long.

The Millau Viaduct

The Tarn Valley is a wide river gorge in France, with high plateaux on either side. The valley is crossed by a major highway connecting Paris with Barcelona in Spain, and it is a busy link for holidaymakers journeying from the north of France to holiday resorts in the south. For years, traffic would grind to a halt as cars made their way along winding roads into the town of Millau and over a bridge crossing the River Tarn. Because of the lengthy delays and growing air pollution, it was decided that a new route had to be built – and so began the Millau Viaduct.

When engineers looked at the site, there seemed to be several ways to go about this project. They could tunnel through the hills on either side of the Tarn and connect the road with smaller bridges across the valley. But tunnelling is expensive, so they came up with another option – a bridge across the entire valley, from plateau to plateau.

The bigger bridge proved to be the best solution, but it would have a huge impact on the landscape. So, instead of simply handing the design over to engineers, the British architect Lord Norman Foster

WORD ORIGIN

plateaux
viaduct

was commissioned to design a structure that would blend in with the environment as well as being useful.

He decided the bridge should look as delicate and transparent as possible, as if it had risen out of the land – more like a sculpture than a piece of engineering.

The engineering company Eiffage was chosen to turn his blueprint into reality.

River Tarn

Millau Viaduct   Millau

FRANCE

KEY

| ■ | A75 – the new highway |
| ■ | N9 – the old road |

QUESTION

Why do you think Lord Norman Foster wanted to keep the bridge as delicate and transparent as possible?

. . . but it would would have a
huge impact on the landscape

The Millau Viaduct

The result is the world's tallest bridge – it is even taller than the Eiffel Tower and, at 2.4 kilometres long, it is the world's longest cable-stayed bridge. The structure is supported by seven concrete piers, unlike most bridges, which have only two or three. The masts rising above the deck and cable stays down the middle of the bridge are made of steel.

The deck, or road-bed, of the bridge is also made out of high-grade steel, instead of the usual concrete. This not only made it lighter but also meant that the minimum amount of material was used in its construction.

Eiffage built the deck at their factory in 2000 separate pieces, and brought it to the site to be assembled.

The "lighter" steel deck still weighed 36,000 tonnes, so moving it into place was a major feat of engineering. Temporary support towers were built between each pier to help support and position the deck. The force used to push the deck out into space, from pier to pier, came from a hydraulic lifting system. The builders used the global positioning system (GPS) to make sure the deck was placed exactly as it should be, while hydraulic rams shifted the deck forward at a rate of six metres every four minutes.

INFERENCE

What inferences can you make about . . .
The builders used the global positioning system (GPS) to make sure the deck was placed exactly as it should be?

...it is the **world's longest** cable-stayed bridge

The Millau Viaduct was constructed over a period of 32 months.

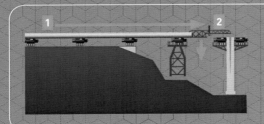

1 The hydraulic lifting system moves the concrete deck from pier to pier.

2 The deck sags as it moves between each pier. The hydraulic lifting system lifts and pushes it to the next pier.

Temporary support towers were built between each pier.

CLARIFY

stays
feat
GPS

QUESTION

What questions could you ask about the construction of the Millau Viaduct?

GENERATE

Seven concrete piers were constructed to support the weight of the bridge.

The Millau Viaduct curves slightly, allowing better visibility for drivers.

MILLAU VIADUCT

Total length of the deck	2.46 kilometres
Number of piers	7
Shortest piers	77 metres
Highest piers	240 metres
Thickness of the deck	4.20 metres
Width of the deck	32.05 metres
Total volume of concrete	85,000 cubic metres
Weight of the metal structure	36,000 tonnes
Total weight of bridge	290,000 tonnes
Construction period	32 months
Total cost to build	390 million euros

The Millau Viaduct was constructed from the outside in, so that the two middle ends were finally joined.

To reduce the effect of wind on drivers, side screens were added to the bridge.

... it didn't look too **imposing**
on the landscape

Using steel meant that, although the bridge was very strong, it didn't look too imposing on the landscape. But what about the motorists using the bridge? How would driving at a height of over 300 metres above the ground affect them? Winds at this altitude can sometimes reach speeds of 150 kilometres per hour, making the short journey across potentially hazardous. So side screens were added to the bridge, reducing the wind by up to 50 per cent.

The height of the bridge plus the distance across the gorge could also cause drivers to feel as if they were floating in space. For this reason, the bridge curves slightly across the valley, which not only makes it look graceful, but also gives drivers better visibility.

After the Millau Viaduct was completed in December 2004, motorists driving south could trim hours off their travel time. Though it takes only a minute or so to drive across, the Millau Viaduct is fast becoming a tourist attraction in its own right.

MILLAU VIADUCT

KEY POINTS	INTERESTING FACTS
The Millau Viaduct was built to link Paris and Barcelona.	Lord Norman Foster decided the bridge should look as delicate and transparent as possible.
?	**?**

VISUAL CHALLENGE

In what other ways could you present this information?

CLARIFY

hazardous
visibility

The Channel Tunnel

The English Channel between England and France is one of the busiest shipping waterways in the world. Freight ships and ferries carry large numbers of passengers back and forth across the channel every day.

Sea travel in the English Channel can be unpleasant and dangerous. More than 20 gale-force storms rage there every year, and ferry passengers often suffer from seasickness. Dense fog is also common, and has caused many fatal accidents.

For more than 200 years, people talked about building a safe, easy and quick way for people and goods to cross the channel. Finally, in 1987, the British and French governments agreed on a proposal to build a train tunnel from shore to shore beneath the sea.

PREDICT

What challenges do you think engineers might face in building a tunnel across the English Channel?

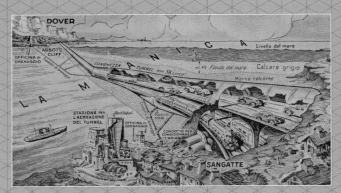

An Italian idea for the Channel Tunnel from 1949.

In 1914, at the start of World War I, this suggestion was put forward for a tunnel to allow the King of England to travel to Paris.

. . . sea travel in the English Channel can be unpleasant and dangerous

An aerial view of a ship on its side in the English Channel. This ship collided with another ship in thick fog.

INFERENCE

What can you infer about . . .
For more than 200 years, people talked about building a safe, easy and quick way for people and goods to cross the channel?

BRITAIN

Folkestone

Coquelles

FRANCE

The Channel Tunnel links England and France.

This photograph shows a 1935 shipping disaster in the English Channel involving a French cruise liner.

Ferries carry passengers back and forth across the English Channel.

CLARIFY

fatal

QUESTION

Why do you think a service
tunnel was constructed?

Tunnelling under Castle Hill, Folkestone.

One of the of five tunnelling machines used in France to dig the Channel Tunnel.

The Channel Tunnel is actually three tunnels – two rail tunnels and a third smaller service tunnel between the other two. The rail tunnels can carry three types of trains – high-speed passenger trains, shuttle trains for cars, trucks, buses and their passengers and freight trains. People quickly nicknamed it "the Chunnel".

The engineers planned to use a type of excavator called a tunnel-boring machine, or TBM for short. A TBM is 250 metres long and has a cutterhead that is nearly nine metres wide. It can eat through five metres of rock in an hour. The machine is designed to carry away the cut rock, called spoil, and to place concrete segments that line the tunnel walls. But first the engineers had to decide on the best place to dig.

Digging a tunnel through soft, crumbling soil or sand can be very difficult because of the danger of collapse. Digging underwater is almost impossible as workers are likely to face unexpected floods. So engineers worked with geologists to find the best path for the tunnel.

The seabed is made up of many layers of different types of rock laid down over millions of years. The engineers and geologists were interested in a thin layer of rock called chalk marl, which is sandwiched between layers of weak rock. Chalk marl is ideal for tunnelling because it is soft and easy to cut, yet strong and waterproof.

They made bore holes in the seabed and studied the rock, tracing a wrinkled, 20-metre-thick line of chalk marl. But they also found fissures where seawater had seeped into the chalk marl. The first several kilometres on the French side showed several serious fissures which engineers had to analyse and repair before tunnelling could start.

INFERENCE

What inferences can you make about the importance of geologists in planning the Channel Tunnel?

. . . people quickly nicknamed it
"the Chunnel"

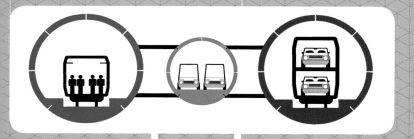

The Channel Tunnel consists of three tunnels:	
	a tunnel with trains carrying passengers
	a service tunnel
	a tunnel with trains carrying cars, trucks, buses and their passengers, and freight trains

When the digging began, the path the TBMs would follow had been carefully mapped out. The British brought in massive pumps in case they needed to pump out seawater in an emergency. The French used special TBMs because they knew that they would sometimes be working in very wet conditions as they burrowed under the sea.

Like most tunnels, the Channel Tunnel was dug from both sides at the same time. This speeds up the time needed to complete the tunnelling and shortens the distance that the spoil has to travel to be carried away. The workers don't need to travel as far for fresh air or emergency services. The most difficult challenge is to make sure that the two tunnels meet in the middle.

TBMs cannot back up to make corrections in their path. The engineers calculated that both tunnels would line up – horizontally and vertically – within a metre of each other. The engineers knew that no single tool could guarantee a perfect meeting, so satellite and laser technology were used. Satellite information helped place the tunnels horizontally, but couldn't help much with the vertical position. Laser guidance systems proved hard to use in the cramped, undersea conditions.

CLARIFY
technology

INFERENCE

What inferences can you make about the conditions when tunnelling started?

The removal of debris and water was an ongoing job during the construction of the Channel Tunnel.

QUESTION

Why do you think the spoil from the TBM machine had to be carried away?

. . . to make sure that the two
tunnels meet

The tunnel was dug from both sides at the same time.

Celebrating the breakthrough on 28 June, 1991.

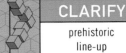
CLARIFY
prehistoric
line-up

CHANNEL TUNNEL

Total length of the tunnel	50 kilometres
Average depth under the seabed	45 metres
Number of tunnels	3
Diameter of main tunnels	7.6 metres
Diameter of service tunnel	4.8 metres
Total amount of soil removed during building	8 million cubic metres
Date tunnelling started	1 December, 1987
Date tunnel opened	6 May, 1994
Estimated total cost to build	£10 billion

A freight and vehicle train passing through the Channel Tunnel.

A passenger train arriving in France at Coquelles after the 35-minute journey through the Channel Tunnel.

An aerial view of the Channel Tunnel entrance near Folkstone in England.

The engineers also had another way of checking their tunnelling progress. Workers on the TBMs sent out drill probes 200 metres ahead of the cutterhead to take samples of the chalk marl. Geologists working on the TBMs looked at the samples under microscopes and identified the shells of prehistoric animals. They knew which animals could be found in each part of the chalk marl, so they could tell the engineers how to adjust the path of the TBMs.

After two and a half years of non-stop tunnelling, there was great excitement as two workers chipped through the last bit of chalk marl with hand drills. When the rock fell away, French and British workers clasped hands through the narrow linking hole, 40 metres below the English Channel seabed.

Measurements showed that the horizontal line-up was accurate to approximately 8 centimetres and the vertical line was accurate to 25 centimetres. This incredible achievement made it possible to walk between Britain and France for the first time since the end of the last Ice Age – about 8500 years ago.

Two more tunnels had to be completed before the Channel Tunnel opened in May 1994. At 50 kilometres long, it is the longest underwater tunnel in the world. Millions of people and vehicles now travel under the English Channel, at an average depth of 45 metres beneath the seabed.

CHANNEL TUNNEL

KEY POINTS

In 1987, the British and French governments agreed on a proposal to build a train tunnel from Britain to France.

INTERESTING FACTS

?

VISUAL CHALLENGE

In what other ways could you present this information?

Taipei 101

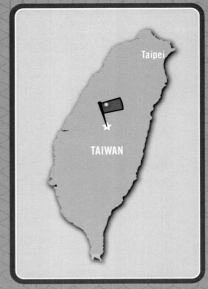

Taipei 101 is situated in Taipei, Taiwan.

Taipei is the capital of the island of Taiwan. It is a wealthy, booming city with the second highest population density in the world. Six million people live in and around it. With so much pressure on the available space, often the only way to build is up. As Taipei grows, so does its skyline.

In 1999, work began on Taipei 101. At more than half a kilometre high, it is the tallest building in the world. Inside are shops, restaurants, offices for 12,000 people and the Taiwan Stock Exchange. It was designed to remind people of Taiwan's native bamboo plant. Taipei 101's main floors are grouped into eight sections of eight floors each. Eight is a lucky number in traditional Chinese culture – it represents "blooming" or success.

Constructing a building of this size meant there were some big problems to overcome.

INFERENCE

What can you infer about Chinese culture from ...

Eight is a lucky number in traditional Chinese culture – it represents "blooming" or success?

Crowds of people at a shopping mall inside the Taipei 101 tower.

Taipei 101 under construction.

PREDICT

What do you think some of the big problems in constructing Taipei 101 might have been?

Taipei 101 rises high above the other buildings in Taipei, Taiwan.

The remains of a six-storey building in northern Taiwan. It collapsed after heavy flooding caused by a typhoon.

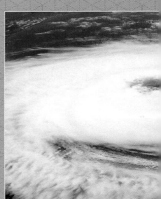

This satellite view shows a typhoon developing.

Earthquakes in Taiwan have caused many fatalities and massive structural damage to buildings.

Taiwan sits on a geological fault line in the Pacific Ocean, a position that means that earthquakes are certain to happen sooner or later. Taiwan is also prone to typhoons, with wind speeds of 120 kilometres or more. So Taipei 101's engineers had to plan for the worst. They decided to design the building to stand up to the strongest earthquake that could possibly happen in a 2500-year cycle.

An earthquake occurs when there is sudden movement along a fault in the earth's crust. The movement creates energy that travels through the ground in waves. These waves cause the earth to shake, rock and heave violently in many directions. When the waves hit the ground under a building, the building starts to shake, too. These waves find the weak spots in a building and can cause it to collapse.

OPINION

Do you think any building could completely withstand an earthquake? Why/why not?

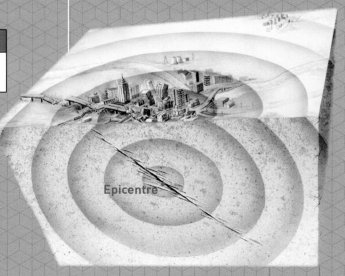

Epicentre

A cutaway of an earthquake. Earthquakes create energy that travels through the earth in waves, causing it to shake. When the waves hit the ground under a building, the building begins to shake.

Taipei 101's engineers knew that a building will be weak if some parts of it are more stiff, strong or flexible than others. They needed to find a way to make the strength of the building the same from bottom to top. To solve their problem, they came up with a unique solution: megacolumns.

Each side of the super structure has two megacolumns that are 22.5 metres apart. The megacolumns are connected to a core corner column by floor girders, or horizontal supports, forming a pattern like a noughts-and-crosses board.

The megacolumns are strong. They are made of steel that can be 8 centimetres thick. Up to level 62, they are filled with reinforced concrete that is twice as strong as the concrete used in most skyscrapers. In all, 90,000 tonnes of steel connect the megacolumns to the building's core.

Connections are especially important in buildings that need to stand up to earthquakes. Strong, flexible parts are useless if they are not joined together properly. Metal parts are joined together by applying heat and pressure in a process called welding. Usually, two pieces of metal are welded together by "melting" the surface of each piece and pushing them together. However, Taipei 101's engineers decided on a slower, stronger method called full-penetration welding. This meant that each piece was heated right through before they were pressed together. Choosing this method caused enormous delays and skyrocketing costs.

INFERENCE

What inferences can you make from . . .
Strong, flexible parts are useless if they are not joined together properly?

The erecting and welding of the steel columns proved to be a very slow and costly process.

CLARIFY

megacolumn

Various stages
of Taipei 101
construction.

TAIPEI 101	
Height of building	509 metres
Weight of building	700,000 tonnes
Number of storeys	101
Construction period	1999-2004
Approximate cost to build	$1.7 billion

Taipei 101's dampers were assembled on site.

Taipei 101's dampers can be locked down when needed.

A building that is 101 storeys tall moves in the wind – even with the strongest structure and the best connections. This sway, or vibration, is normal, but people living and working in a super-tall building often find the gentle sway uncomfortable or disturbing.

To reduce the sway, the engineers designed three motion-absorbing attachments called dampers. Visitors to the building can see the biggest of these – a 660-tonne ball, six metres in diameter, made of 12.5-centimetre-thick layers of steel. The ball hangs from steel cables at level 92 of the building and takes up five floors. As the ball swings with the wind vibrations, giant shock absorbers convert the motion energy to heat energy and calm the building's sway. Two more dampers control the movement of the 60-metre-tall pinnacle above the building's 101st floor.

All the dampers are designed to be locked down in the event of an earthquake or typhoon. When that happens, the building will rely on its megacolumns to withstand the shocks. Designed to resist the effects of earthquakes, typhoons and its own towering height, Taipei 101 is the ultimate super building.

CLARIFY
pinnacle
locked down

QUESTION
Why do you think people in Taipei 101 might find a gentle sway uncomfortable?

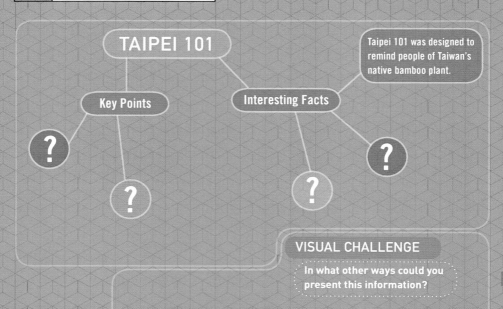

TAIPEI 101

Taipei 101 was designed to remind people of Taiwan's native bamboo plant.

Key Points

Interesting Facts

?

?

?

?

VISUAL CHALLENGE
In what other ways could you present this information?

Super Challenges

There are super structures all over the world, and each was built to meet certain needs and overcome certain challenges.

- The largest hydroelectric power plant on Earth is the Itaipu Dam. It was built from 1975 to 1991, and more than 30,000 people were involved in the construction of the dam. It harnesses the power of the Parana River on the Brazilian-Paraguayan border and provides millions of people with electricity.

- The CN Tower is the world's tallest free-standing structure. It is used as a telecommunications transmitter and is thought to be a signature landmark in the city of Toronto, Ontario. It is possible to see approximately 100-120 kilometres from the top of the tower, on a clear day

- Until recently, the Golden Gate Bridge in San Francisco was the world's tallest suspension bridge. It was built in 1937 and has a distinctive art deco look. It is still one of the longest bridges and is considered to be one of the most beautiful bridges ever built.

- The Western Deep gold mine in South Africa is a network of tunnels that travel 3.5 kilometres deep into the earth's crust. It is a dangerous place to work, and many miners die each year. Engineers are planning to build the Western Ultra-Deep Levels, which will reach a depth of five kilometres. This new shaft is due for completion by 2009.

- The Shanghai Express is the world's first commercial maglev, or magnetically levitated train. It carries travellers 30 kilometres in seven minutes and 20 seconds, at speeds of up to 431 kilometres per hour.

- The International Space Station orbits 360 kilometres above Earth. The first section of the station was taken into space by shuttle in 1998, and it has had a changing crew of three since 2000. Sixteen countries have worked together to build this scientific base on the frontiers of space.

As the world's population continues to grow, the super structures of the future will have to do more.

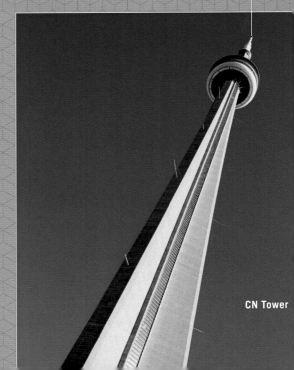

CN Tower

SUPER CHALLENGES

⦿ KEY POINTS

INTERESTING FACTS

?

?

VISUAL CHALLENGE

In what other ways could you present this information?

Shanghai Express

Itaipu Dam

International Space Station

INDEX

Think about the Text

**Making connections – what connections can you make
to the information explored in Super Structures?**

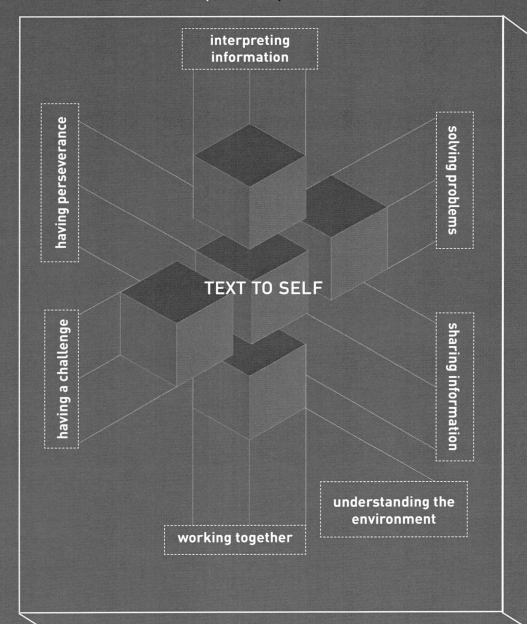

interpreting
information

having perseverance

solving problems

TEXT TO SELF

having a challenge

sharing information

working together

understanding the
environment

TEXT TO TEXT

Talk about other informational texts you may have read that have similar features. Compare the texts.

TEXT TO WORLD

Talk about situations in the world that might connect to elements in the text.

Informational Report

1 Organise the information

Select a topic:

Super Structures: List the things you know and what things you will need to research.

What I know:

- People have built super structures for many hundreds of years.
- Architects, engineers and builders are some of the many people involved in building super structures.
- Super structures can include bridges, buildings, tunnels, dams, etc.
- Many different types of materials are used to build super structures.

What I will research:

- How, where and why are super structures built?
- What are the materials used in the construction of super structures?
- What types of structures are there?

2 Locate the information you will need

- Library
- Internet
- Experts

3 Process the information

Skim-read.
Sort your ideas into groups.
Make some headings.

4 Plan the report

Write a general introduction.

6 Write up your information

5 Decide on a logical order for your information

What will come first, next . . . last?

7 Design some visuals to include in your report

You can use graphs, diagrams, labels, charts, tables, cross-sections . . .

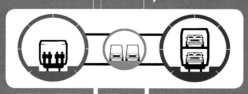

The Channel Tunnel consists of three tunnels:		
	a tunnel with trains carrying passengers	
	a service tunnel	
	a tunnel with trains carrying cars, trucks, buses and their passengers and freight trains	

WRITING AN
Informational Report

HAVE YOU . . .

- recorded important information?

- written in a formal style that is concise and accurate?

- avoided unnecessary descriptive details, metaphors or similes?

- used scientific or technical terms?

- written a logical sequence of facts?

- avoided author bias or opinion?

Don't forget to revisit your writing. Do you need to change, add or delete anything to improve your report?